Baby's First Merry Christmas

# Christmas Tree

**Bauble**

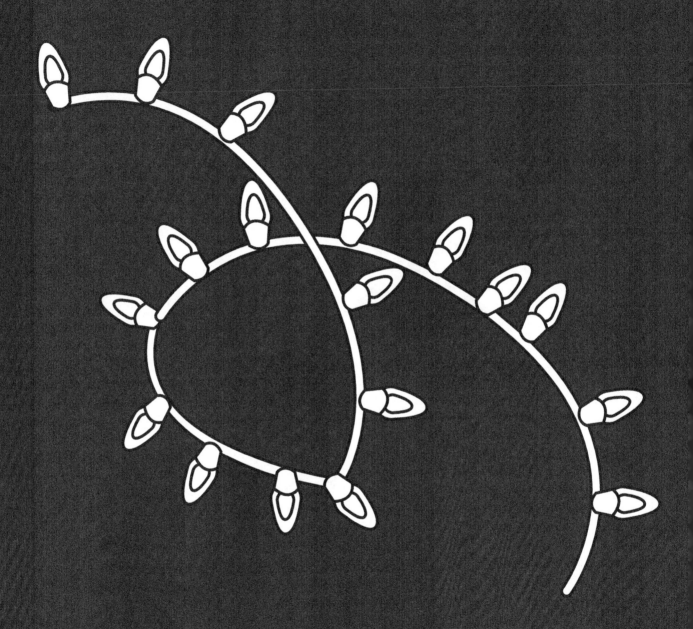

**Christmas Lights**

Christmas Present

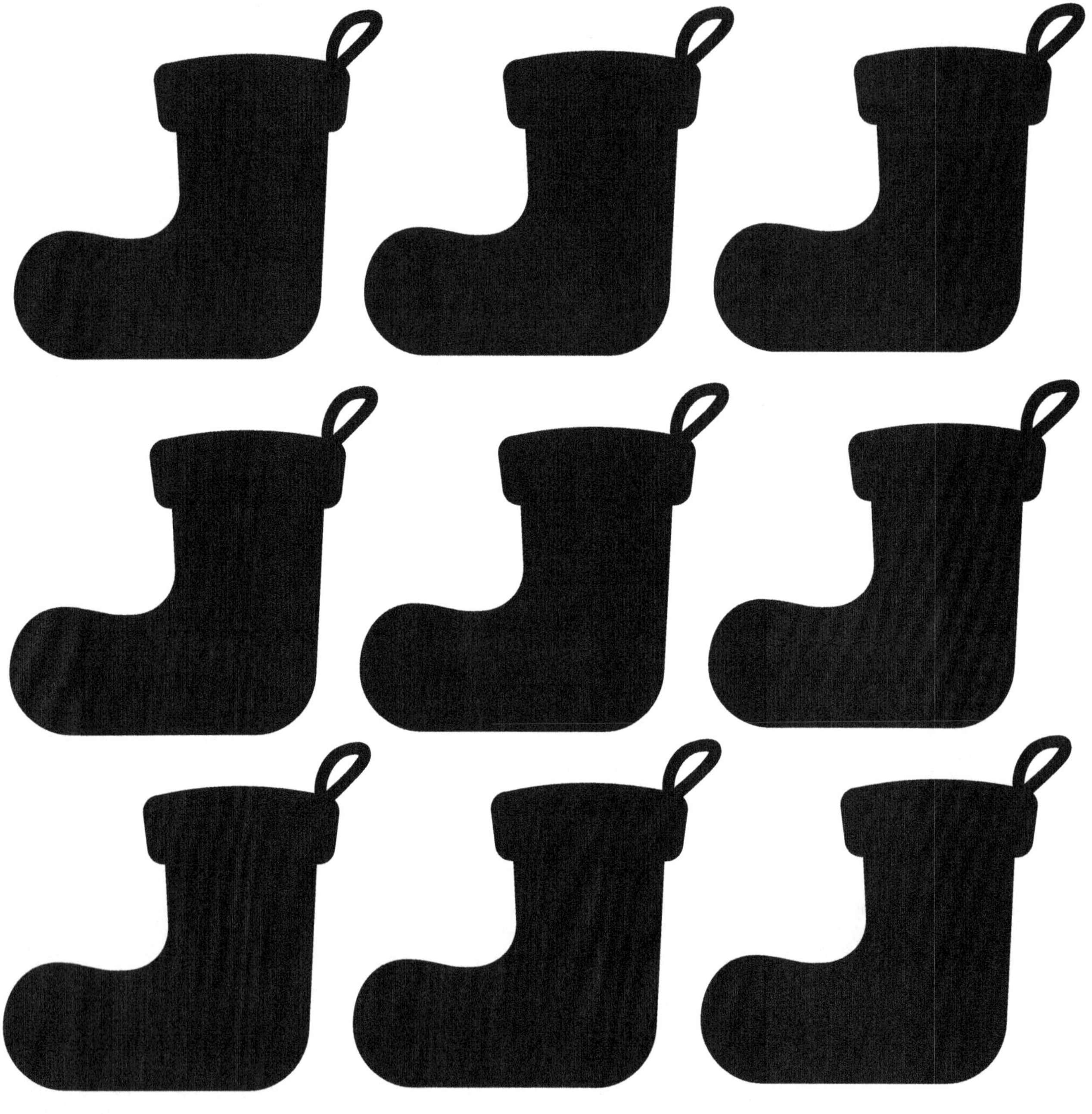

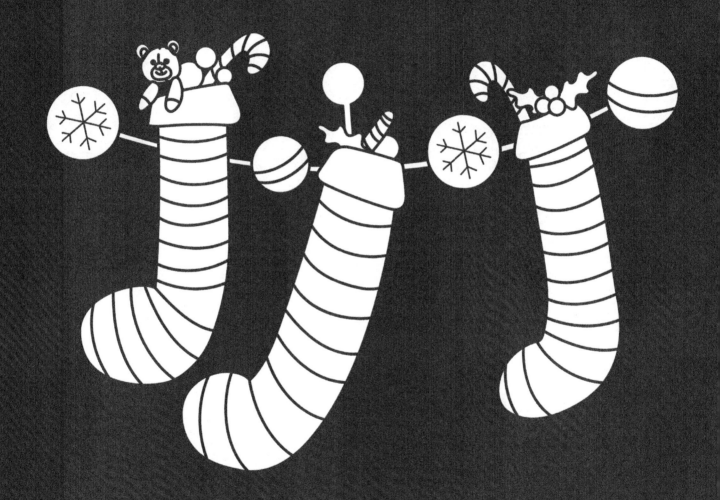

# Stockings

Santa Claus

# Reindeer

Elf

# Gingerbread House

# Gingerbread Man

# Candy Cane

# Christmas Cake

**Wreath**

# Holly

Snowflake

**Snowman**

# Polar Bear

Penguin

# Dinosaur

Truck

Printed in Great Britain
by Amazon

12407249R00025